How to Read Music

Beginner Fundamentals of Music and How to Read Musical Notation

By: Erich Andreas

ISBN: 978-1492783527

First Printing, 2015

Printed in the United States of America

Terms of Use

You are given a non-transferable, "personal use" license to this product. You cannot distribute it or share it with other individuals.

Also, there are no resale rights or private label rights granted when purchasing this document. In other words, it's for your own personal use only.

Table of Contents

Quick Summary

The ability to read music is a POWERFUL skill set that allows musicians to turn a lifeless piece of paper with dots and lines into beautiful, living/breathing music!

It's somewhat of a lost art in this "learn it quick" technology-driven time that we live in. HOWEVER, for those that take the time to master its principles, reading music will allow them to INSTANTLY play music that they have never heard before.

As you may know from my videos at http://www.youtube.com/yourguitarsage, http://www.yourguitarsage.com and http://www.unstoppableguitarsystem.com, I am a BIG fan of **playing music by ear.**

However, there is nothing like sitting down with a piece of sheet music and playing music from a whole different perspective. It's VERY exciting and I promise that if you take the time, you will reap GREAT rewards from understanding this method of digesting music.

There are a few different levels of reading music, with each requiring a different dedication level.

The first level is the basic understanding of rhythms, note locations and their values. That is, when you see a note on the "staff", you can identify it and THEN find it on your instrument.

The second level is actually being somewhat proficient and being able to "size up" a piece of sheet music before you begin, work out the bits that are difficult and then read/play the music after a few times through.

The third level is typically attained by symphony/orchestra/pit musicians who have been reading/playing for a while. High school band members will have to have some ability to read and this venue is great for gleaning musicians into this 3rd level, but it DOES take much dedication.

The first time I experienced a musician with that caliber of reading level, I was learning the solo for Bark At The Moon (BATM), by Ozzy Osborne. I was reading tab, as musical notation does not typically denote which frets should be played (only notes). My girlfriend at the time was 1st violinist in the Nashville Symphony and was PHENOMENAL at sight-reading music. I asked her to play a very fast phrase from that solo and without blinking she played it BETTER than I did after about an hour of sitting with the tablature.

SO, you can see just how powerful this skill actually is. It's a different way of thinking. We are using a different part of our brain and looking at music from a totally different angle.

It's slow for EVERYONE at first, but in time you WILL get quicker.

I want you to think about a small child for a minute and his/her ability to communicate before EVER going to school. It's said that a four-year old has a vocabulary of about 1,400-1,500 words before starting kindergarten. How is that?

They have learned by ear, which is how many musicians learn to play. However, this child learns to read around this age and is not very good at first. In fact, they are terrible at reading.

But wait Erich!

They are just kids, they need time to learn. Give them a chance. They are not terrible they just need to read more.

Do you see what I just did there?

Instead of preaching to you about practicing and that learning to be proficient at sight-reading music takes time and dedication, you instead told ME that.

SO, remember this! Just like that child who at 4 years old did not know how to read, at 5 years old learned how to read VERY slowly, at 6 years old was reading much quicker and by college was going for his/her doctorate, YOU TOO, will go through these stages. That is UBER-important to remember! Because, WHEN you get frustrated that you are not moving along quicker, you WILL be tempted to quit. And I DON'T want that happening!

Remember that EVERY new skill takes some time to learn. It's not you going slow, it just takes some time.

Have fun with this!

It's a lot like learning a new language. You will be clunky and slow at first, but in a short while, with dedication and practice you will be speaking the language of music with proficiency!

Now let's do this!

From the Author of the #1 *Amazon.com* Bestseller, *Guitar Mastery Simplified*, and *Ukulele Mastery Simplified*.

Erich Andreas

Chapter 1: Introduction

At first, reading sheet music might seem a bit complicated. This is particularly true for guitarists, since they have so many other tools at hand, such as tablature and other resources.

Nevertheless, learning to read sheet music correctly is a very useful tool for a musician, regardless of the instrument that is being played. There is a reason why sheet music has been the dominating form of musical notation for centuries: it is a form that actually takes into consideration the particularities of music as a specific code, not relying on gestures or memorizations – it is actually logic. It is a representation of sounds with symbols that contain a lot of information – including loudness, pitch, duration and timing – in a rather simple system.

The logic that sustains sheet music also enables the musician to have a broader view of the music he is playing, understanding the system behind it. Notes, intervals and chords can be seen more clearly on the staff than on tabs, and this helps the musician develop his musical abilities as well as deliver better music.

As learning any new language, the study of sheet music requires practice and persistence. But once the new knowledge is acquired, it is of great value to the musician.

Chapter 2: Basic Notions of Music

Sound and pitch

As is commonly known, music is made of sound, or more specifically a combination of sounds harmonized in a specific way. But first of all, what exactly is sound?

Sound is caused by the vibration of air molecules, in the form of waves – the *sound waves*. These sound waves are caused by a vibrating object (for instance vocal chords, or the strings of a violin) and expand throughout space, loosing force, as they get farther or hit obstacles. This explains why we find it harder to listen to sounds from afar, or behind walls.

There is **one feature of sound waves** that is of the uttermost importance to music: pitch. Pitch derives from the *frequency* of the sound waves – the number of occurrences of a wave, inversely proportional to wavelength. Consider the following visual example:

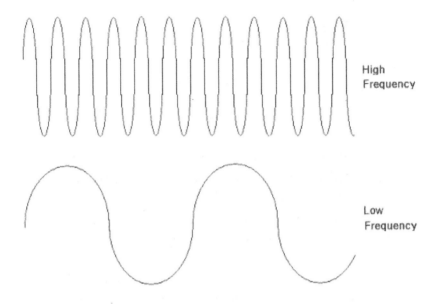

High
Frequency

Low
Frequency

Pitch is therefore the *"perceptual property that allows the ordering of sounds on a frequency related-scale extending from low to high"*(1). In other words, the pitch is the auditory sensation we have of the sound of a certain wave on a certain frequency, which can be classified as "high" (waves with a faster oscillation, that make the air vibrate faster) and "low" (those with slower oscillation).

Timbre

There is yet another trait of sound that is fundamental for the understanding of music – timbre. This characteristic is usually metaphorically described as the "sound's color", and is related to the *source* of the sound wave.

For instance, while a guitar and a piano can play a sound with identical pitch, loudness and duration, they are still easy to distinguish because of the different *timbre* of each of these instruments:

The concept is not explained by any simple acoustic property but depends mainly on the coarse spectral energy distribution of a sound, and the time evolution of this. Whereas pitch, loudness, and duration can be quite naturally encoded into a single scalar value, timbre is essentially a multidimensional concept that is typically represented with a feature vector in musical analysis tasks(2)

In essence, <u>timbre</u> is the *texture* associated with a particular instrument or voice, what makes each one unique. It is determined by various physical characteristics of the sound waves, including spectrum and envelope.

Notes

As observed, there are various sounds that can be created according to their traits, such as pitch, loudness and timbre. Sounds with the same pitch are perceived in a similar way by the human ear, and to these pitched sounds are given the name of notes(3).

The notes are grouped into different pitch classes – sets of all pitches that are a whole number of octaves apart. In other words, these pitch classes include many different pitches with frequencies in a ratio of any power of two. It is important to observe that, in reality, each of these pitch classes has an infinite number of pitches, but the human ear can only hear a limited amount of them. Observe some of the C's included in the pitch class C:

The pitch classes correspond to the traditional names of Do, Re, Mi, Fa, Sol, La, Ti and Do. In most Anglophonic countries, the pitch classes are represented by the first seven letters of the alphabet – A (La), B (Si), C (Do), D (Re), E (Mi), F (Fa) and G (Sol).

It is also necessary to differentiate the many notes contained in a single pitch class, as they fall into different octaves.

To identify each one, the most commonly used system is the scientific pitch notation. In this system, the notation combines the letter of the pitch class (along with eventual accidentals) and a number identifying the octave.

Also, one should take in to consideration accidentals. Accidentals can either be a *sharp #*, or a *flat* ♭ . A sharp raises a note by a semitone, while a flat lowers it a semitone. For instance, F# is a note half-step above F, while A ♭ is half-step below A.

It is interesting to note that some of these accidentals will inevitably create corresponding pitches that are only represented differently. For instance, a D ♭ is equivalent to a C#, and a B# is equal to a C. If we consider all these possibilities of equivalent pitches, we shall discover that the complete chromatic scale has five additional pitch classes from accidentals added to the

seven original ones, adding up to a total of 12 –
each separated by a semitone.

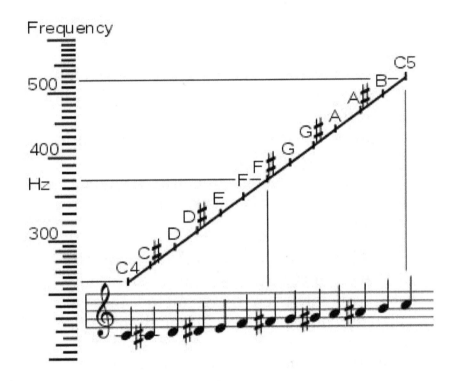

Scales

As seen previously, it is possible to identify octaves equally divided into twelve distinct notes (with different pitches), each separated equally by a half-step (or *semitone*). A scale is a series of these notes, selected by a specific criterion. These scales have notes that are harmonic, and are of great importance for composers to create harmonic melodies.

The scales are ordered according to the pitch of the notes. They are typically listed from low pitch to high pitch – these are called *ascending scales* – although there also are *descending scales*. Most scales are also *octave-repeating*, which means that their pattern of notes can be repeated in every octave – this also means that this scale can exist in different pitch levels of octave.

The most common sort of scale used is the diatonic scale – basically, the major scale and the natural minor scale. The diatonic scales have eight notes (seven notes and an eighth note that repeats the first, only an octave higher), which are separated from each other by five whole steps and two half-steps. Therefore, the half-steps might be separated from each other by either two or three whole steps.

Following this specific pattern, it is easy to notice that the succession of natural notes – A-B-C-D-E-F-G – is a diatonic scale, as is any transposition of it – such as C-D-E-F-G-A-B.

The white keys of a piano were designed to play the natural notes; therefore, playing the white notes in succession results in a diatonic scale. For instance, we can build a major scale on the piano if we start on the C key, and continue on to the next keys to the right:

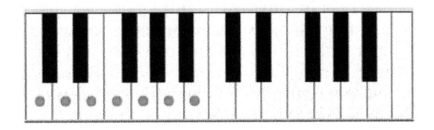

If we start on the A key, and follow the same instruction, a natural minor scale is built:

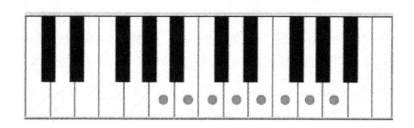

It is important to note, however, that we distinguish between major scales and natural minor scales not by the note on which they are begun, but by the pattern on which they are built – more specifically, the separation between each note in whole steps (tones) and half-steps (semitones).

The major scales are defined by the following intervals, with "W" standing for "whole-step" and "H" standing for "half-step": W-W-H-W-W-W-H. **A scale** is named after the note on which it begins. Therefore, let us construct the C major scale step by step for better understanding:

First note (called *tonic*): C

Second note (called *supertonic*): a whole step above C is D

Third note (called *mediant*): a whole step above D is E

Fourth note (called *subdominant*): a half step above E is F

Fifth note (called *dominant*): a whole step above F is G

Sixth note (called *submediant*): a whole step above G is A

Seventh note (called *leading tone*): a whole step above A is B

Eighth note (called *octave*): a half step above B is C

As we had anticipated, the final note of the scale is also C, an octave higher than the initial C.

It is important to note that the C major scale is the most simple of all, as it does not require any sharps or flats. Let us observe the A major scale, using the same pattern. To simplify the construction of the scale, the notes are "in parenthesis", while the whole steps and half steps separating them are **bold**:

(A) **W** (B) **W** (C#) **H** (D) **W**
(E) **W** (F#) **W** (G#) **H** (A)

As stated beforehand, this scale uses sharps (which could be replaced by flats), as do all the major scales aside from C major. We can see the major scales represented in the following chart:

	C	C#/Db	D	D#/Eb	E	F	F#/Gb	G	G#/Ab	A	A#/Bb	B
Db	7	1		2		3	4		5		6	
Ab	3	4		5		6		7	1		2	
Eb	6		7	1		2		3	4		5	
Bb	2		3	4		5		6		7	1	
F	5		6		7	1		2		3	4	
C	1		2		3	4		5		6		7
G	4		5		6		7	1		2		3
D		7	1		2		3	4		5		6
A		3	4		5		6		7	1		2
E		6		7	1		2		3	4		5
B		2		3	4		5		6		7	1
F#		5		6		7	1		2		3	4

For each major scale, there is a corresponding natural minor scale, yet it starts on a different note – more specifically, it starts on the sixth note (or *submediant*) of the major scale. It is easy to understand this relation to the major scales once we observe the sequence of intervals that define the natural minor scale: W-H-W-W-H-W-W. As one might infer, the sequence is very similar to that of the major scale, except the last two intervals (a whole step and a half step), that should be placed between the sixth and seventh notes and then the seventh and eighth notes, are in the beginning of the sequence. Graphically, we can describe this as follows:

Pattern For Major Scales

W - W - H - W - W - W - H

Pattern For Minor Scales

W - H - W - W - H - W - W

These natural minor scales have a relation, therefore, as with each one of the major scales, they are often called relative minor scales. To better analyze the minor scales, let us use the relative minor to the major scale we analyzed, C major. The sixth note of C major scale is A. Therefore, let us build the A minor scale step by step:

First note (called *tonic*): A

Second note (called *supertonic*): a whole step above A is B

Third note (called *mediant*): a half step above B is C

Fourth note (called *subdominant*): a whole step above C is D

Fifth note (called *dominant*): a whole step above D is E

Sixth note (called *submediant*): a half step above E is F

Seventh note (called *subtonic*): a whole step above F is G

Eighth note (called *octave*): a whole step above G is A

Once more, as we had anticipated, the final note on the scale is also A, an octave above the A on which the scale was initiated.

Of course there are other kinds of scales aside from the diatonic scales. Another sort of scale that is important for this initial approach on musical scales – and which we have already mentioned previously – is the chromatic scale.

A chromatic scale has a total of twelve pitches, separated by exactly one half step each (one half step above for ascending scales, and one half step below for descending). The most important thing in chromatic scales is that as there is perfect symmetry between all the notes – the notes are all equally spaced – there is no tonic, and therefore it is a *non-diatonic scale.*

Another symmetrical scale is known as the whole tone scale, on which the notes are separated by a whole step from one another. Once more, the equal distance between the notes means there is no tonic in the scale.

The three types of scales analyzed so far – chromatic, whole tone and diatonic scales – are classified according to their patterns, or the intervals between their notes. Another way of describing scales is according to the number of pitches included in an octave of a scale.

For instance, the major scale contains eight notes, but the final note is one octave above the first. Therefore, in a single octave, the scale has seven notes – and is consequently called a *heptatonic scale*.

It is common that different musical genres use different sorts of scales, that vary in complexity and possibilities of composing. While the *heptatonic scale* is the most commonly used in Western music, jazz usually works with *octatonics* (which have 8 tones per octave), while Western folk music uses *hexatonics* (6 tones) or *pentatonics* (5 tones).

As mentioned before, scales are very important for composing as they are responsible for bringing harmony into the melodies. Scales are also the basis for the construction of chords.

Chords

Chords are important for musical students in general. When a single sound of a specific pitch is played once (think pressing one key on the piano or stroking a single string of the guitar), a note is played. If 3 or more notes are played at *the same time*, it is a chord.

In essence, a chord is a *"combination of three or more pitches sounding at the same time"*(4).

In Western music, the most commonly used chords are the *triads*, chords made up by three notes, although there are chords with different numbers of notes. These notes are selected using the various degrees of the scales, so that the chords are harmonic. Therefore, chords can have different chordal qualities according to the scales from which the notes were selected. For instance, there are *major chords* as well as *minor chords*.

As an example, let us take a *major chord*. We should form the C major triad from the C major scale. As we have seen previously, the C major scale consists of: C-D-E-F-G-A-B. A major triad always consists of the first, third and fifth notes of the major scale. So, the C major triad should be C, E and G played simultaneously.

On the piano, the C major triad should look like this:

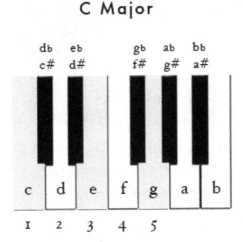

On the piano it is simpler to visualize the chords, as the notes are keys that should be played. Playing all of the keys equivalent to the notes enables us to play the chords.

On the guitar, the musician must hold down the strings so they sound like the correct notes – C, E and G. So, on the guitar, the C major triad looks like this:

In the picture above, the fingers are pressing the second, fourth and fifth strings, according to the scheme below (the note letter names above the strings show the note name played in the chord NOT the open string):

C MAJOR CHORD

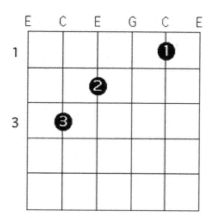

On the guitar it is more difficult to visualize the notes – but each specific point where the fingers press on each specific string sounds as a different note. When playing the guitar, it is important to remember that the distance between one fret and the next is a half step. Every time the guitarist slides his finger an extra fret up (towards the bridge), the pitch goes up one half step.

With that in mind, it is possible to analyze the C major triad on the guitar. To do so, let's remember the guitar strings' original notes, when none of the strings are pressed down:

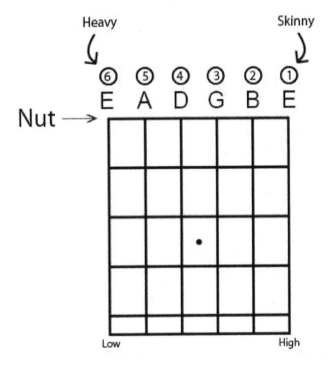

Now, we can analyze all the strings, one by one, and understand exactly what notes are being played:

    • String 1: E string played open   =
E

    • String 2: B string played at the first fret (+1 half step)   = C

• String 3: G string played open   =
G

• String 4: D string played at the 2nd fret
(+2 half steps)   = E

• String 5: A string played at the 3rd fret
(+3 half steps)   = C

• String 6: E string played open   =
E

As this illustration shows, when playing the C major triad on the guitar, the notes being played are always either C, E and G – the three notes extracted from the C major scale. So, although the notes are not as visible as on the piano, the logic behind the chord is the same.

Let us do the same with a *minor chord*. Minor chords are also formed from the first, third and fifth notes of the *minor* scale. We have already defined, when studying scales, that the A minor scale is A-B-C-D-E-F-G. So, the A minor triad should be A, C and E played simultaneously.

On the piano, the A minor triad looks like this:

A Minor

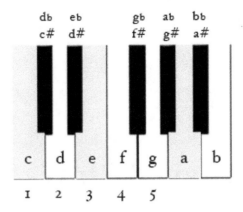

On the guitar, it should look like this:

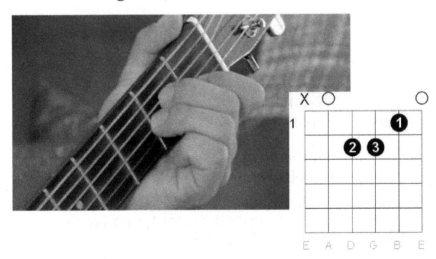

Chapter 3: How to Read Music

The Musical Staff

First off, to learn to read musical notation it is important to understand the support on which the notation is built on. Thus, the first element we must analyze is the musical staff, also called musical stave.

The musical staff is a set of five horizontal lines, on which symbols are placed to represent notes, chords and even pauses. The staff should be always read from left to right, and from the top of the page to the bottom.

Aside from the horizontal lines, the musical staff should have some vertical lines that divide it into sections. These lines are called bar lines, while each section is called a measure. The function of these measures is organizing the music into beats.

The bar lines can also have different utilities, according to the way they are depicted.

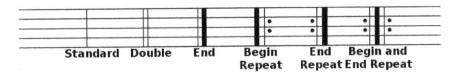

While a simple (standard) bar line separates the measures, the double bar line marks the end of the piece or of the song. The bar lines that appear with double dots mean a certain part of the song must be repeated – the section between the "begin repeat" and the "end repeat" should be repeated a single time.

Clefs

On its own, a musical staff does not represent any specific notes – in other words, it is not previously decided that notes placed at any particular line of the staff represent specific notes. For this, it is necessary to place clefs, or musical symbols used to indicate the pitch of the notes written on the staff.

There are two main clefs: the *treble clef* and the *bass clef*.

The *treble clef* is typically used for instruments that play on a higher pitch, and is commonly also called G-clef(5). It is placed with its curve passing over the second line(6) of the staff, as showed below:

When the treble clef is placed on the staff, it is possible to discern the notes according to their location on the staff lines: the note placed on the second line will always be G, and all the others will be defined according to their relation (distance) to G. In accordance to this, let us observe the C major scale on a staff with a treble clef:

C D E F G A B C

The *bass clef* is commonly used for instruments that play on a lower pitch. If these instruments were to use the treble clef for their notation, the lower notes (which they use with greater frequency) would appear so below the staff that it would be difficult to read them. As occurs with the treble clef, the bass clef is frequently referred to as F-clef(7). It is placed with the fourth line of the staff between its two dots, as illustrated below:

When the bass clef is placed in the musical staff, the note represented on the fourth line is always F, and all the other notes can be distinguished according to their distance to F.

There is also a third kind of clef, called the C-clef. The C-clef always indicates where the middle C is placed.

There are two C-clefs that are currently used: the *alto clef*, when the C-clef is placed on the third line of the staff, and the *tenor clef*, when it is placed on the fourth line.

Time Signature

The time signature is a symbol of great importance when reading music, as it states how many and what kind of notes per measure there are. It is written along with the clef, at the beginning of the musical staff, and looks like a fraction.

The top number of the time signature always shows how many beats are in a measure. The bottom number shows what kind of note will be equivalent to a beat: 1 represents a whole note, 2 represents a half note, 4 for a quarter note, 8 for an eighth note and 16 for a sixteenth note.

Simplifying, the time signature shows whoever is reading the music sheet how many of which note will be used in each measure. The most popular time signature nowadays, used for pop and rock music, is 4/4. So, what does 4/4 mean? It means that the song uses 4 quarter notes per measure.

It is possible to exemplify with other cases: for instance, the ¾ means there are 3 quarter notes per measure, while the 5/2 means 5 half notes per measure, and so on.

It is also quite normal to encounter a symbol called *common time,* similar to a letter "c", which is equivalent to 4/4:

Notes

As seen up to now, on most of the contemporary music sheets, notation on music staffs would either be treble clefs or bass clefs to determine the notes on it.

The position of the notes on the musical staff aids us to determine their pitch: as notes are written closer to the top of the staff, they have higher pitches, whereas when they are on the bottom, the pitch is lower. As we have also said, the staff with a treble clef usually displays notes on a higher pitch, while lower notes are usually shown on bass clef staffs. As some instruments have a wide range of notes to suit different pitches, such as the piano, they can use two staves combined, one with each of the clefs. When they are shown together, they are united by a brace, and we call the unity a *grand staff.*

It is also important to note that, in some occasions (actually quite frequently) a note's pitch is not depicted on the musical staff, so the note is shown below or above the staff. When this occurs, a small line is drawn with the note, so it is possible to understand its exact position (and, therefore, pitch). This small line is called a ledger line.

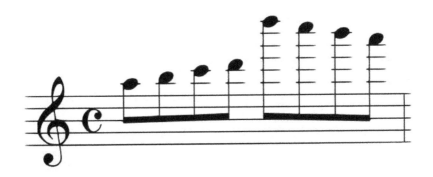

While the position of the note expresses its pitch, the way the note is represented shows the reader its duration. Each note of different duration – whole note, half note, quarter note, eighth note and sixteenth note – is represented by a slightly different symbol.

As we have seen before, the time signature determines how many of a specific note there should be per measure. In the 4/4 time signature, there should be 4 quarter notes per measure. The quarter notes – also called *crotchets* – are represented by a filled circle, with a vertical line attached to it:

Accordingly with the time signature, there are four quarter notes in each measure of the song.

As for the other notes: a whole note –
called a *semibreve* – is always represented by an
unfilled circle without the vertical line attached.
As it corresponds to four quarter notes, there
should be a single whole note per measure:

Obviously, this also changes the duration
of the note when playing the song – the whole
note should have four times the duration of a
quarter note.

A half note – also known as a *minim* – is
represented also as an unfilled circle, with a
vertical line attached to it:

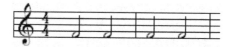

As each half note has the same duration as
two quarter notes, it is natural that there are two
half notes per measure.

As for the eighth notes and sixteenth
notes, they are represented differently as they
can be shown individually or in groups of 2, 3 or
4. The eighth notes – called a *quaver* – are
represented by filled circles, which have a
vertical line as well as a single curl off that line
attached to them. When they are shown in the
groups aforementioned, a single horizontal line
unites the group:

As for sixteenth, or *semiquavers*, they are also shown as filled circles with a vertical line, but have double curls off the line. Also, when they are joined in groups, a double horizontal line unites them:

On the previous diagrams, the eighth and sixteenth notes were not placed on the 4/4 time signature musical staff. To do so, all it is required is to remember that every 2 eighth notes and every 4 sixteenth notes should require the same amount of time as a single quarter note – therefore, each measure should contain either 8 eighth notes or 16 sixteenth notes:

Besides these basic note durations, there are also the dotted notes. The dots serve to add additional duration to the basic notes – each dotted note has an additional duration of half of the original note (in other words, a dotted note equals 1 ½ time duration of the original note).

The dot is always placed to the right, next to the note:

Accidentals and Key Signature

So far, we have seen that the position of a note on the musical staff represents its pitch (among the notes A-B-C-D-E-F-G), and the way it is drawn on the scale shows its duration. Now let's look at how to register accidentals on the staff.

As one must remember, accidentals can be either a *sharp #*, that raises the note a semitone, or a *flat* ♭ , that lowers it the same amount.

The symbols for accidentals are always represented *to the left* (before) each note. Observe the example:

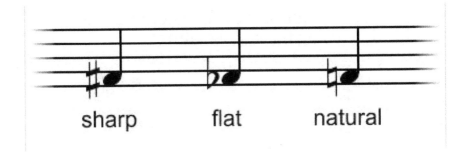

sharp   flat   natural

It is important to remember that not all songs are played in C major – and, according to what we have seen previously in scales, the C major scale is the only major scale that does not contain any accidentals. Considering that, we might infer that a song in any other major scale would be full of accidentals, and therefore would be very confusing to read. To illustrate this, here is the B major scale registered on a musical staff:

There is, however, a specific tool to avoid this problem: the key signature. Much like the *clef* and the *time signature*, the key signature is information that comes at the beginning of the musical sheet that informs us that notes in specific positions are accidentals.

The key signature is the placing of the accidental symbol on or between the lines where the note will always be an accidental. It always appears after the clef, and before the time signature.

Here is the scale of B major once more, this time using the key signature:

Notice that the second note is placed on the space reserved for C (between the third and fourth line), but as in the key signature there is a sharp # symbol in the same space, every time a note appears there it should be read (and played) as C#.

Finally, among the accidental marks there is also one called natural. The natural is used when, after placing a key signature, a certain note placed on a flat or sharp space/line should be played natural. For instance, a natural would be placed if a note that -- according to the key signature – would be played B# should actually be played B.

Rests

Asides from notes, another important kind of symbol used in musical notation are rests. Rests mark moments in which the instrument should not be played, a pause in the music.

There is one rest equivalent to every note in duration, or in other words, rests have the same duration spans as notes: a whole rest, a half rest, a quarter rest, an eighth rest, sixteenth rest, etc.

The whole rest is represented as a dark rectangle attached to the line of the staff, facing *downwards*:

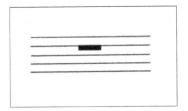

The half rest is very similar; it is also shown as a dark rectangle attached to the line, yet facing *upwards:*

It is very important to stress the difference of the whole rest and the half rest, as their similarity might be confusing and might affect the rhythm of the song being played. As stated previously, while the whole rest faces *downward*, the half rest faces *upward*.

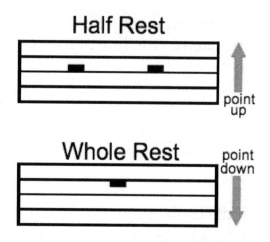

The quarter rest is depicted by a vertical curl, resembling a "curly line:"

The eighth rest is shown as a slanted line with a single dot beside it:

And the sixteenth rest is depicted in a similar way to the eighth: it is shown as a slanted line, with a double dot beside it.

Here is a brief reminder of the different types of notes and rests, so we can move on to the next subjects:

Name	Note	Rest
Whole Note	𝅝	
Half Note	𝅗𝅥	
Quarter Note	♩	
Eighth Note	♪	
Sixteenth Note	𝅘𝅥𝅯	

Dynamics

We have seen that there are ways to show the pitch and duration of each note – but we still have not discussed how to infer *loudness* from the musical sheet.

This is where *dynamics* come in. The symbols of dynamics alter the *volume* in which the music is played. This volume is related to the *intensity* of the playing, and not exact volumes in decibels – so it is also related to the musician's interpretation of the song.

There are various ways of expressing the dynamics in a song. One of them is by words or letters, in a system that varies from *Pianissimo* (the softest) to *Fortissimo* (the strongest):

- *Pianissimo* → *pp* → very soft, very quietly
- *Piano* → *p* → softly, quietly
- *Mezzo-Piano* →*mp* → somewhat quiet, moderately soft
- *Mezzo-Forte* → *mf* → somewhat loud, moderately strong
- *Forte* →*f* →strong, loudly
- *Fortissimo* →*ff* → very strong, very loud
- *Sforzando* → *sfz* → a sudden accent

○ *Forte Piano* then quiet   → *fp* → loud and

Aside from the use of these words and letters, the accent can also be expressed with the use of the symbols *crescendo* (gradually louder) or *diminuendo* (gradually quieter). These symbols are positioned under the staff, as shown in the figure below (the *crescendo* symbol is to the left, and the *diminuendo* is to the right):

All these symbols – the letters, names and *crescendo-diminuendo* can be used in the same song to show the variations of volume in a same piece.

It is important that the musician takes into consideration how to play each volume in the context of the song. Some songs have greater dynamic variations – they can vary from *ff* to *pp*, for instance – and, as expected, the nuances between similar dynamics, such as *ff* and *f*, will be very discrete, and they will be hard to distinguish. In pieces where there is very little variation, the nuances are clearer.

Articulation

There are still other symbols that influence the reading of music from music sheets. These are called *articulation* symbols, and they refer to the transition or continuity of a single note or multiple notes of the song.

The slur, for instance, shows that certain notes should be played without separation, in a single "breath", forming a single musical phrase. Specifically for the guitar, it indicates that the notes should be played *without plucking individual strings*. The slur is depicted as a curved line that embraces the notes, which is usually placed over the notes if the stems are pointed downwards, but can also be under the notes in case the stem is facing upwards.

The tie looks very similar to the slur, but instead of connecting many different notes it only connects two of more notes of the same pitch. It indicates that these notes should be played as a single note, in one "breath".

As said, there are some articulation symbols that indicate to play a single note with more emphasis when compared to those around it. These are called accent marks.

In the image above, from left to right, are shown the accent marks, symbols for *staccato, staccatissimo, martellato, marcato* and *tenuto*.

The *staccato* symbol indicates that the note should have a shortened duration followed by a brief silence that separates it from the following note. In other words, the note should be played abruptly, markedly separated from the others.

The *staccatissimo*, as one might imagine, is the superlative of the *staccato*. The same effect is repeated in a more exaggerated way. The notes should be clearly separated from the rest.

The *martellato* is used only when playing bowed string instruments (such as the violin). It indicates a specific effect that is obtained by pressuring the bow against the string.

The *marcato*, sometimes popularly referred to as *accent*, shows that a certain note (or chord) should be played louder and harder than the surrounding notes. This is one of the most common articulation symbols. The *strong marcato*, a superlative of the same effect, is often depicted with the symbol ^.

The last of the symbols depicted, the *tenuto*, alters the dynamics and duration of a note, generally meaning to hold the note in question slightly longer.

There are also anti-accents, symbols that also modify a single note compared to the surrounding notes, but not as emphasis. These are usually used in percussion.

The three symbols depicted indicate the same effect, in different levels: playing the note softer than the surrounding notes. The first one (where a symbol similar to the letter "U" is placed over the note) means it should be played slightly softer; the second (with the note placed in parenthesis) means it should be played significantly softer; and the third (with the note placed between brackets) means it should be played very soft.

Another very important articulation symbol is the *fermata*, also called *birdseye, hold* or *pause.*

This symbol, always placed over a note or a pause, indicates that it should be sustained for longer than its value would indicate – exactly how much longer is a decision that is up to the performer or conductor.

Last but not least, there is yet another articulation symbol of great importance for guitar players, as it is a technique used frequently with this instrument: damping, also known as choking. This is basically the technique where the sound of a note is interrupted by stopping the strings from vibrating. It can be done in two different ways: either by *palm muting* the strings (pressing the picking hand gently against the strings in order to stop the vibration) or by *fret hand damping* (loosening the fingers on the left hand, so there is less pressure on the strings and they cease to vibrate).

In musical notation, damping is represented by a symbol that resembles a square without the fourth side:

Ghost Notes

Ghost notes, also called dead notes or false notes, are a concept especially important for those learning to play the guitar. Ghost notes are notes that have a rhythmic value, but no discernible pitch. On the guitar, this would be a note or chord played with muted strings.

It is usually represented by an "X" instead of the circle that usually represents the note, although it might also be depicted by placing the note in parenthesis (as the anti-accent mark).

For better understanding of the use of the mark, here is a musical staff with ghost notes for bass, along with the corresponding tablature:

Chords

As we have analyzed previously, chords are 3 or more notes (selected from scales) that are played simultaneously. We have also seen that the most common type of chord is the triad, a chord formed by three different notes.

The chords are represented on the music exactly as what they are: three notes played at the same time. Therefore, to represent notes being played simultaneously, one should represent them above/below one another.

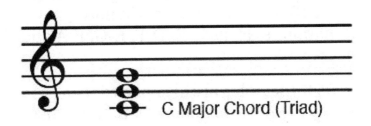

C Major Chord (Triad)

So when three or more notes are placed together, they form a chord depicted on the musical staff.

Intervals

Aside from chords, there are some important intervals that would be good for us to identify. The word intervals, actually refers to the ratio between two notes on a scale, but it is also often used in reference to a combination of two notes that respect this ratio.

Thirds are one of the basic types of intervals. In thirds, notes are separated by three or four half steps. So, when choosing two of these notes on a scale, they should be chosen "skipping every other note" for instance, the first and the third notes of the scale, the second and the fourth, and so on(8).

If we build thirds on a C major scale (C-D-E-F-G-A-B), for instance, we will find combinations such as C-E, D-F, E-G, F-A and G-B.

As these notes are also played simultaneously (as are chords), they are also represented above/below each other. Here are the thirds for the C major scale:

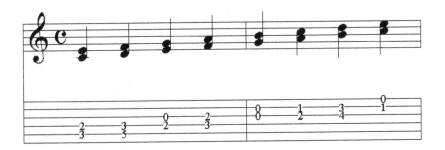

One should notice that, since these notes are always at least a whole tone apart, they never *overlap* each other, although there is no space between them. Every time a third is depicted, it will look like this: two notes together, not overlapped, but with no space between them.

Another important interval is the seconds. Seconds are notes separated only by one or two *half steps*. This means that, on a musical scale, they are a combination of a note with the following note. Here are the seconds for the C major scale:

Differently from the thirds, the depiction of the seconds shows two notes that do overlap one another, as they are so close together.

The fourth has five or six half steps between the two notes, which means that when choosing them from the scale, it is necessary to "skip two notes". So, on the C major scale (C-D-E-F-G-A-B), some possible fourths would be C-F or D-G, for instance. Here are the fourths for the C major scale:

As they have the 5 or 6 half steps between them, the notes will always be depicted in the same way: one on the line, the other between the lines, and with a half space between the notes.

Last, the fifth has 6 or 7 half steps between the notes. As a result, either both notes will be depicted on lines, or both will be between lines, and there will be a full space between them.

Chapter 4: Counting

Beat and Counting

As we have seen previously, musical notation brings a series of information about the song to the musician: *how many* notes should be played, their *pitch*, their *loudness*, their *duration*, and their *intervals*, among others.

Yet, to fully understand music sheets and to play music from them correctly, it is important to understand *when* to play each note: for this, there is a technique called "counting".

Counting is related to understanding the rhythm of the song, and also understanding the duration of each note. So, first of all, we must remember the symbols that represent each note duration:

Name	Note	Rest
Whole Note	𝅝	
Half Note	𝅗𝅥	
Quarter Note	♩	
Eighth Note	♪	
Sixteenth Note	𝅘𝅥𝅯	

As mentioned earlier, each note has a different *duration*, and the amount of each of these notes will vary according to the *time signature* defined at the beginning of the music sheet.

When counting, a musician is actually counting the *beats*. But what is a beat?

In music theory, a beat is the basic unit of time, as a pulse. Beat is directly connected to the *rhythm*, as this is formed by a sequence of stressed and unstressed beats.

The counting of beats in a song depends on its *time signature*. To learn to count here, we will use the 4/4 time signature, which is the most common in music.

In the 4/4 time signature, we will consider that each measure will have *four beats*. So, if we also take into consideration that each measure can have four quarter notes, it is pretty obvious that each quarter note will last one beat.

Let us see how this works out for all different kind of notes:

English names for notes and rest values

Sign	Name	Relative Length	In $\frac{4}{4}$ Time	Rest
o	Semibreve	Whole note	4 beats	—
♩	Minim	Half note	2 beats	—
♩	Crotchet	Quarter note	1 beat	𝄽
♪	Quaver	Eighth note	½ beat	𝄾
♪	Semiquaver	Sixteenth note	¼ beat	𝄿

It might seem confusing that the note that is equal to a whole beat is a "quarter note", while the "whole note" is actually four beats. It's easier to think that, in this time signature, *each measure has the time of a whole note.* So, a quarter note can be called a quarter because it takes a quarter of the measure.

Counting is *actually* counting the beats in each measure, to understand how long each note should take. In the following example, for instance, in the first measure we have a whole note, so it should take all the four beats. To play it, we should count 1-2-3-4 as evenly spaced as possible.

1 2 3 4   1 2   3 4   1   2   3   4

In the second measure, there are two half notes – so each of them has two beats. So we should count 1-2 for the first note and 3-4 for the second.

The third measure has all four quarter notes, so each has a single beat. So we only have to count one beat for each note.

In counting, one of the most important aspects is that the "numbers" are evenly spaced. If they are not, you won't be playing "in time". One way to keep time is by tapping your foot in a steady fashion.

Now we have seen what happens when we count whole notes, half notes and quarter notes. When we move on to eighth notes and sixteenth notes, things get trickier, as they will require more than a single note per beat.

For eighth notes, each note takes only ½ beat. This means that we need to add an extra note for every number we count. Musicians usually do this (at least at the beginning) by counting 1 + 2 + 3 + 4 + (reading the "+" as "and"). So you would say "1 and 2 and 3 and 4 and", taping your foot on each number. Your foot would come up on the "ands". This is the upbeat.

The same logic applies to the sixteenth notes; only you need extra "words" – these notes require only a fourth of a beat, so each beat should have four of them. One common way of doing this is saying the letters "E" and "A" in addition to the number and the word "and". It should sound something like "1 E and A, 2 E and A, 3 E and A..." and so on. Of course, one can choose other words or letters, as long as they are small enough to keep all of them equally spaced (and the rhythm correct). When tapping your foot to sixteenth notes, you would still use the same method as eight notes and quarter notes (tapping ONLY on the numbers).

Observe below the equivalence in beats of each kind of note, on the musical staff:

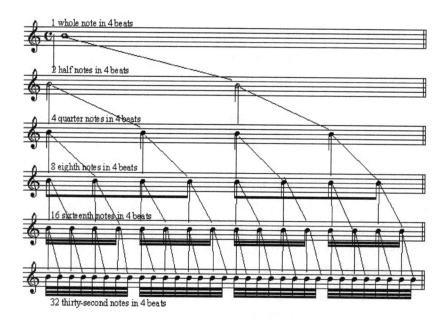

Overall, counting requires a lot of practice, especially the fast counting required for the eighth and sixteenth notes.

Of course, the measure will not always be shared among notes of the same kind – and if the notes do not have the same duration, the way the beats are shared is also unequal.

In the following example, one half note and two quarter notes are in the same measure:

As we have stated before, the half note takes *two beats*, and each quarter note takes a *single beat*. When practicing, one should count 1-2-3-4, tapping their foot on the numbers ONLY.

The more varied the notes, the more challenging it becomes to count. In the next example, we have three different kinds of notes: one quarter note, one half note and two eighth notes:

Here, the quarter note takes one beat, the half note takes two, and the two eighth notes together take the last beat.

The counting rules also apply to *rests*, except instead of playing the instrument

65

during the counting, one should <u>not</u> play. Here is an example:

In this example there is a quarter note and a quarter rest – each taking a *single beat*. Following that are three eighth notes (which take 1 and ½ beat), followed by an eighth beat (the remaining ½ beat).

It seems very complicated at first, but counting is mainly a matter of practice. Over time, the counting process becomes so natural that the musician does not need numbers or words to aid her, being able to do all the counting in her own head.

Tempo

Lastly, let's discuss "tempo". The concept of tempo is often confused with that of beat, but they are actually different ideas in regards to musical theory (although directly connected).

The tempo appears at the "top" of the music sheet, and is measured in *beats per minute.*

This might seem difficult at first, but there are tools to help musicians count these beats according to the appropriate tempo. The most commonly used is the metronome, a device that ticks on a regular basis indicating the beats precisely to the musician.

Summary

Does your brain hurt yet? I KNOW! That was a LOT of information in a short amount of time, but I have purposely presented this information to you in this way so that you get the facts and get to reading some sheet music.

However, congratulations are in order because you now know more about reading music then about 90% of the musicians out there.

ALSO, remember the stages that a child learns to communicate and read. Before reading this book you knew how to play by ear. Now you are like that child who has just learned the alphabet and the sounds of the vowels and consonants and how those letters are put together to form words.

If you remember from kindergarten, children of that age have a hard time assembling words because they're still thinking about the letters. Once they get that skill down, they start thinking about the words and not the letters so much anymore. Then again with time they see phrases instead of words. You too will progress in this fashion on your journey of music.

Remember, take your time, be patient with yourself and practice a lot! You are learning a new language.

NOW, there are a myriad of apps and websites that will allow you to view sheet music and try your hand at reading. So go read some music!

Thank You

Before you go I would like to say a big "thank you" for purchasing and reading my book.

I know you could have easily purchased someone else's book on how to read music. But you took a chance with my book.

Huge thanks for purchasing and finishing the entire book.

If you liked this book then I need your help real quick!

Please take a few moments to leave your review for this book on Amazon.

http://www.yourguitarsage.com/reading-music-book-review

Your feedback will continue to help me provide you and everyone else with more music books. And if you really liked it then please let me know. :)

One Last Thing My Friend...

If you feel like other people could benefit from the material that is in this book then feel free to share it with your friends.

Thanks again!

http://www.facebook.com/yourguitarsage

http://www.twitter.com/yourguitarsage

A Cause Close to My Heart

As many of you know, I am a BIG animal lover and advocate for animal welfare. I also believe to be of great significance in this world, we need to leave more than we have taken and we MUST take a stand for those that don't have a voice. Two things that I have always been passionate about are guitars and animals. If you have a heart for animals like I do, you will be happy to know that a portion of every YourGuitarSage purchase is given to animal welfare organizations like: http://www.nokilladvocacycenter.org and http://www.tribeofheart.org

Many people have not taken the time to understand the gravity or plight of many of the animals living in our world today. Since the cause is so big, I have focused my cause on the issues of "spay and neuter" and animal cruelty prevention through legislation, law enforcements and education. "Spay and neuter" is also known as animal population control or the sterilization of domesticated (house) pets and feral (wild) animals where necessary and able. It's a simple procedure that can save millions of animals' lives every year from the carelessness/cruelty of "unconscious" humans.

Here are some basic facts to show you just how quickly one cat or dog left to breed can have a DRASTIC impact on the death toll.

Cat		Dog	
1st year	3 litters = 12 offspring	1st year	4 offspring with 2 females
2nd year	144 offspring	2nd year	12 offspring
3rd year	1,728 offspring	3rd year	36 offspring
4th year	10,736 offspring	5th year	324 offspring

If you are a pet owner, I IMPLORE you to spay/neuter your animal. This is an EASY way to change 1000s of innocent lives. Oh yeah, and Karma will shine upon you :)

Also, if you feel moved to do so, please give to the organizations above. Together, we have the power to change this world! Please join me!

Erich Andreas

Resources

<u>Other Books by Erich Andreas</u>

#1 *Amazon.com* Bestseller – *Guitar Mastery Simplified*

http://www.GuitarMasterySimplified.com

Amazon.com* Bestseller – *Ukulele Mastery Simplified

http://www.UkuleleMasterySimplified.com

<u>Getting Started Playing Guitar – Free Video Course (25 Videos)</u>

http://www.GettingStartedPlayingGuitar.com

<u>Your Guitar Sage - Free Guitar Ebook</u>

www.YourGuitarSage.com

<u>The Unstoppable Guitar System</u>

How to Master Your Right and Left Hand Techniques – Free Video Course

http://www.unstoppableguitarsystem.com/

Your Guitar Sage Videos

http://www.youtube.com/yourguitarsage

Your Uke Sage

http://www.yourukesage.com

YouTube/yourukesage

http://www.youtube.com/user/yourukesage

Bibliography

1) Anssi Klapuri, Manuel Savy (2006). *Signal processing methods for music transcription.* Springer, p. 8.

2) *Ibid.*

3) In some contexts, "note" refers to the sign used in musical notation to represent a sound with specific duration and pitch. We shall analyze this use of the word furthermore.

4) Benward; Saker (2003). Music: In Theory and Practice, Vol I, p. 359.

5) It is important to note that although the *treble clef* is often seen as a synonymous for G-clef, they are not actually the same. The treble clef occurs when the G-clef is placed specifically at the second line of the staff (always counting from the bottom to the top), and is currently the only G-clef still in use. Therefore, it is possible to note that the treble clef is a G-clef, but not all G-clefs are treble clefs.

6) When counting the lines of the staff, it should always be done from the bottom lines to the top lines.

7) Once more, the confusion of *bass clef* with F-clef is erroneous. As occurs with the treble clef, the bass clef is the only F-clef that is still in use,

although in the past there were other F-clefs such as the *baritone clef* and the *sub-bass clef*. Therefore, the bass clef is only one of the many kinds of F-clefs.

8) In reality, this is a simplification of the concept of a third, as will also be done to the concept of the next intervals, used to introduce the reading of these intervals on the music sheet. It ignores the existence of minor and major intervals, as well as the construction of these intervals based on the chromatic scale, focusing instead on extracting them from diatonic scales.

Britannica Encyclopedia, 1992. Vol. XXIV, "Music", p. 493.

Benward, Bruce & Saker, Marilyn (2003). *Music: In Theory and Practice,* Vol. I.

Randel, Don Michael (2003). *The Harvard Dictionary of Music.*

Taylor, Eric (1989). *AB Guide to Music Theory.*

Wikipedia.org

CPSIA information can be obtained
at www.ICGtesting.com
Printed in the USA
BVHW061108020520
579070BV00012B/2299